UNDER LOCK AND KEY, HONOR AND OBEY PART 1

AIJA M. BUTLER

UNDER LOCK AND KEY, HONOR AND OBEY PART 1
AIJA M. BUTLER

Copyright© 2013 AMB Publishing-Aija Butler

All rights reserved, including the right to reproduce this book or portions thereof in any form whatsoever. Including photocopying, recording, or by any information storage and retrieval system, without permission in writing from the copyright owner.

PAPERBACK VERSION 2013

ISBN-13: 978-0615935713
ISBN-10: 0615935710

Some names and identifying details have been changed to protect the privacy of individuals.

We have tried to recreate events, locales and conversations from memories of them. We may have changed some identifying characteristics and details such as physical properties, occupations and places of residence.

UNDER LOCK AND KEY, HONOR AND OBEY PART 1
AIJA M. BUTLER

Cover design Copyright © 2013 by AMB Industries/AMB Branding and Design

Book design and production by Aija M. Butler

Cover Model: StarKing-TheGod

Editing by LJ Thomas

Facebook: Aija AMB Monique

Twitter: @ambmonique

Instagram: @ambmonique

UNDER

LOCK

AND KEY

"HONOR AND OBEY"

UNDER LOCK AND KEY, HONOR AND OBEY PART 1
AIJA M. BUTLER

THE CONFESSION~KEYSHIA

THE INTERROGATION~BAM

KEYSHIA~GIRL DISTURBED

THE BEGINNING

9 TO 5

BOY FRIEND UNKNOWN

FRIEND OR FOE

TOO MUCH TOO SOON

ALONE AT LAST

THE FAMILY

LOCK~HIGH ON KEYSHIA

UNDER LOCK AND KEY, HONOR AND OBEY PART 1
AIJA M. BUTLER

SHOWERED WITH GIFTS

10…9…8…7…6

DO OR DIE

UNDER LOCK AND KEY, HONOR AND OBEY PART 1
AIJA M. BUTLER

THE

CONFESSION

KEYSHIA

UNDER LOCK AND KEY, HONOR AND OBEY PART 1
AIJA M. BUTLER

"You asked to see me, counselor? I'm confused we aren't scheduled until Thursday."

"I'm not sure where we should start. The nature of this conversation is somewhat delicate. I am going to need your full cooperation." The counselor responded, as he placed an open file onto his desk.

"Ok?" Keyshia said questioning the Doctors interests. Keyshia swung her huge tote back to the front of her as if protecting herself from a possible blow to the stomach, as she took a seat on the couch.

"I think it's best we start from the beginning, don't you?"

"I'm sorry. I don't follow."

UNDER LOCK AND KEY, HONOR AND OBEY PART 1
AIJA M. BUTLER

"I think you do. I understand there was a shooting in at your apartment."

Keyshia looked down at her tote bag and began searching her school books as if looking for an answer. "Oh that! I don't know anything. My head is still very cloudy, with regards to the events of that night. I can still hear the ringing in my ears. The gun fire was in such close proximity. You know if I find anything out or hear something I will most definitely be in touch." Keyshia grabbed for her belongings, and stood instantly in an attempt to flee the counselor's office. All she could think of was getting the hell out of dodge. She didn't want to say anything that would implicate her in the shooting.

UNDER LOCK AND KEY, HONOR AND OBEY PART 1
AIJA M. BUTLER

"Sit down Keyshia!"

Keyshia became instantly lethargic. She was shaking like a leaf and mumbling incoherently.

"Start talking!"

Keyshia looked down at the floor. She then rubbed her arms as if she felt a cool breeze whisk around her and stifle her lungs. Keyshia's chest began to heave and she became anxious with worry. "Are the doors locked? Do you have extra security here?" Keyshia jumped up and ran to the window to ensure there were no predators.

"You are safe here." The counselor spoke softly.

"There was a quiz each night. A physical test of loyalty, or something. Here take this money. You take this money and deliver it... 45 minutes. I counted each dreadful second from damn near Pasadena to Inglewood. Gun exercise, empty the clip and reload... 30 seconds." Keyshia's mind drifted. Tears flowed to her eyes.

"I got used to sleeping with a nice nickel plated 9mm with a beautiful ivory bone handle...safety off...

BUT, content with death.

I can still feel the snap of my arm being jerked outward in my attempt to flee his wrath. I raised my right arm to shield myself from the blow. Catching my arm in midair he assured me that everything was ok and he was not angry.

I came from under my ball of defense and relaxed my strained muscles only to catch the full blow of his furry.

My head jerked back and hit the stone fireplace. The shock of the beating numbed the pain. It wasn't until he said he was sorry that my bones began to ache. During the hours we had company in my dorm apartment he would make a point to show how obedient I was.

He fed upon his desire to create fear in the hearts of his followers. He was short in stature, but he was grizzly. Days drifted into weeks. He worked the dark streets of Los

Angeles. He smelt of trash, when he returned, still he held a hubris fortitude. Happy to see that he had retained ownership, of my person and loyalties, he would dare others to look at me.

If he caught site of such betrayal and possible lust after what he proclaimed to own, he would beat the man senseless then pull a knife and put it to my throat. The same question was always asked, "Do you think I should kill him?"

I would suggest that he be exiled from the group, a small act of courage to protect him from this demons wrath.
God knows my time was near. I too, had plans of making an escape.

UNDER LOCK AND KEY, HONOR AND OBEY PART 1
AIJA M. BUTLER

He didn't take so kindly to my suggestion. He figured I was looking to save my undercover lover. He gave him a small window to either jump from or be thrown out of. He jumped. The second floor was high enough to break a few bones if willfully fleeting. However to be thrown could end a life intentionally. To jump was best.

Unfortunately, my hour of terror had just begun. He continued his speech to his fellow constituents that cringed with fear, but dare not shut their eyes to visual presentations. As their eyes watered afraid to blink, the tears threatened to call attention to possible weakness. He trailed the knife from under my eye down the outline of my face.

The men took the chance to wipe their mugs and adjust their game countenance.

I was stiff as a board and late answering his repeated question. "Are you afraid of me?"
"No!"

The answer he so loved to hear. If I were scared I wouldn't give him the satisfaction of knowing. I fought back tears as he forced the point of the knife into my cheek.

"Good!" He teased.

Flashing his silver pointed medal around. "Because to kill you would then be justified."

UNDER LOCK AND KEY, HONOR AND OBEY PART 1
AIJA M. BUTLER

He grinned, as he leaned in to kiss my trembling lips. I never understood how killing someone would, unless in self-defense, be justified. My plan. However, I believe that his meaning of justification was in reference to his conscience. I questioned the existence of good beneath his rotting skin. I cringed at the thought of unveiling the maggots penetrating his heart.

My eyes lowered and shifted to view his followers.
I begged for their mercy. I winked at those that had fallen for my sly temptress seduction.

For the life of me I couldn't understand why none of them had taken the opportunity to win back their freedom. I'd given plenty of time and opportunity. Motive floated in the air like a cloud of smoke from an uncontained fire.

Desire caused sweat to bead upon their brows and wet their palms.

"Cowards I screamed!" from my delirious mind. My arms and legs were kicking and flinging as hard and fast as they could in my mind. I burned them with my stares. Some looked away. Others dare not show signs of emotion or disagreement to his performance, for fear they too would be asked to leave. Departure without being formally excused as a group could be fatal. If I had the chance, I'd pull the gun from the hips of one of these sensitive assholes and kill him myself.

Mere boys claiming to be men holstering guns they are afraid to use, but jump up and down in an attempt to prove themselves to another man. A man who is just as afraid as they were. We were under his wrath, the lot of us.
Under lock and key!"

UNDER LOCK AND KEY, HONOR AND OBEY PART 1
AIJA M. BUTLER

THE

INTERROGATION

"BAM"

UNDER LOCK AND KEY, HONOR AND OBEY PART 1
AIJA M. BUTLER

"I don't understand. Why did you need me to come down here?" I told you all what you needed to know. So arrest me and let's get this over with."

"We just wanted to ask you a few questions. Keyshia is here. We had her come down to the counseling office to meet with her counselor. We hope that maybe the shock from the shooting has calmed, and perhaps she can fill in some of the blanks." The detective paused to see if he could read the emotions written on Bam's face, but he held a blank stare.

"What happened to doctor patient privilege? Recording her without her knowledge is illegal."

"Who said we were recording her?"

"You didn't have to, something is going down, though. The good doctor must have agreed to provide you all with something. Or else we wouldn't be here. Look, how can I help you?"

The detective lowered his eyes. He didn't figure on Bam being so smart. The truth was Bam was closest to Keyshia. He helped her on her Psychology homework, walked her to and from classes, and served as her mock audience, when she needed to recite papers or conduct experiments. Bam had become quite the psychologist himself. The detective sighed and sat down before Bam. He put his heavy ashy hand on his chin and just stared at Bam for about ten seconds before he began his line of questioning.

UNDER LOCK AND KEY, HONOR AND OBEY PART 1
AIJA M. BUTLER

The detective could tell that Bam was loyal as hell and he would be hard to break, but he was sure there was something missing from this half-baked confession, Bam kept throwing their way.

"Bam how would you characterize Keyshia's behavior?"

"I love her. Everyone did. There wasn't a man in the family that didn't. She just got too caught up."

"What do you mean?"

"Lock! He was so abusive and controlling. I wanted her to leave. We both did. Justin and I. She had started drinking heavily again. Her mind was as clouded as her judgment. She started to think that everyone was out to get her."

"Who is Justin?"

"He is her best friend, ex-boyfriend of four years. No one in the family knew of his real purpose, but me. Justin and I became close."

"That seems strange don't you think? You secretly in love with Keyshia? Chilling with her ex-boyfriend, and working for her current love. How did that pan out?"

"What do you mean?"

"I mean didn't that make you feel angry, jealous, resentful? I could only imagine how hot my blood would boil. You wanted them both dead right?" The detective moved in close and searched his eyes.

UNDER LOCK AND KEY, HONOR AND OBEY PART 1
AIJA M. BUTLER

Bam began to laugh, showing off his perfect teeth. His eyes sparkled like the diamonds in his ears. His complexion was as smooth as the day he was born.

"Officer?"

"Yes!"

"Get to some questions that actually pertain to the happenings of that night. I am not retarded. Yes I was pissed, daily. I wanted nothing more than to protect and love Keyshia. She was just so damn stubborn. She wouldn't listen to reason. I told her we would be fine together, alone. We could leave. Only she was so loyal to this fool, and she feared he would kill me if he found out the truth about me.

UNDER LOCK AND KEY, HONOR AND OBEY PART 1
AIJA M. BUTLER

We both held secrets. When I met Justin I was relieved. Keyshia isn't this evil, manipulative person. She's sick and she needs help. Lock did this." Bam was growing angry. He clinched onto the arms of the chair so hard his knuckles began to turn white. The detective watched Bam's every emotion carefully.

"Where are your parents Darrin?"

Bam looked up with tears in his eyes. "Dead!"

"How did you meet Lock?"

"The streets. That's where I lived. He took us all in and put us on to selling drugs, but Keyshia took care of us. We all stayed with her. Lock was in and out doing what he did best. Lying and facilitating our every move."

"You do know that Keyshia thinks that you are dead, right? She thinks she killed you, along with the others. We have her here for safe keeping as I told you before. But if we find anything to implicate her, we will have no choice but to arrest her. I know you didn't act alone."

"What! Are you crazy? Let her go! I told you all what you need to know about that night. Does Keyshia sound like a sane person to you right now? Is she locked away? Did you give her, her medication?"

"No!"

"WHAT!!!" Bam stood up! It was like he transformed into some angry beast throwing the table from in front of him and chucking the chair at the magic mirror. "Are you fuckin' kidding me? You will kill her!"

"DETAIN HIM!" The startled detective Monroe ordered, as an assisting officer barged in to help quiet the situation.

"Use force if needed." Detective Monroe said as he rolled up his sleeves, like some tough guy.

"You will send her into a maniac depressive state. During these attacks she is volatile and inconsolable. If she is made to feel threatened or fear of any kind. She rambles and says things that are untrue based on truth. Do you understand me? After which, she will try to harm herself and those surrounding her. I NEED TO SEE HER

NOW!" Bam yelled. He was struggling with the officer, who had now called for back-up. Bam was screaming hysterics and demanding to see Keyshia.

"Relax! Keyshia is fine. We can't allow you to see her."

"She needs me." Bam calmed his voice. She isn't stable. I need her."

KEYSHIA

GIRL

DISTURBED

UNDER LOCK AND KEY, HONOR AND OBEY PART 1
AIJA M. BUTLER

"Remember, you can be erased." That was Lock's favorite quote. Keyshia chuckled slightly as she switched positions in her seat. "It was this stupid scare tactic he used to get me to follow suit."

"And, did it work?"

"Of course. But, I had gotten to the point where death didn't seem so bad. The anticipation of his wrath was often worse than the physical beatings. In all honestly, I often dreamed of killing Lock. The abuse was unbearable. Open murderous threats kept me up at night, hand gripping the butt of a gun. I'd used all of my sick days at work. I spent them at home nursing my wounds. Lock usually was very strategic in his beatings before I lost my job.

UNDER LOCK AND KEY, HONOR AND OBEY PART 1
AIJA M. BUTLER

When I was so battered and bruised underneath my collar, I made attempts to stay home, but he'd tell me to toughen up and get to work. My face later became an open target after the lay-off.

"So the family, was made up of 12 knights you say a Kingdom, a formal gang rather?" the psychiatrist tilted his head as he asked about the general make up of Lock and his crew.

"Yes Lock's heart was a bleeding ulcer." Keyshia responded as she revealed her tattoo to the doc.

"What does that mean exactly?"

"He was a blood, and the 12 men you are referring to were called, the disciples."

Keyshia spoke so softly the psychiatrist had to lean in close to hear what she was saying.

"Ok, so tell me about the key people in this circle, the Family, this Bam person, so on and so forth."

Keyshia began to smile, her cheeks became flushed and she felt as though she were going to faint. She loved Bam. His companionship helped her through many storms. She lusted for him, and partook of him physically, but never had Bam settled in her mind and taken it over. She was loyal to Lock.

Keyshia bit her bottom lip and winced as she tried to get up from her lying position. She was still hurt from the stand-off. Her bandages were due for a change. Keyshia sighed just before making her spill on Bam.

"Bam isn't the person you want. Ghost is. He is extremely shady. He hated me, but with good reason. I knew he was dirty and I had plans of exposing all of his dirty deeds. I'm not saying that I am innocent in all this."

"Okay, so what did you have planned for Lock and the family? Before we get back to Bam of course."

"If only Lock were easily persuaded. Conquering the kingdom would have taken but a day."

"What do you mean?" The counselor interjected.

Keyshia laughed, "It's nothing. Just a little rhyme I made up. "Hey do you have a cigarette?"

"This is a non-smoking building." The counselor retorted.

"Oh yeah, that's right." Keyshia said looking off into the air. "I don't smoke anyway."

Keyshia stood up and began pacing the room and twiddling her thumbs. ***"Lock's ability to read minds by his focus on your eyes was filled with evil lies. He stormed out on me, broke all ties. Left me with thoughts of total demise. I had to fend for myself surrounded by a group of criminal minds."***

"Go on."

UNDER LOCK AND KEY, HONOR AND OBEY PART 1
AIJA M. BUTLER

"I wanted the attention you know. Just attention though. Lock provided for me financially, but mentally he lacked sensitivity. He could be quite charming at times, but those times were often followed by brutal beatings. I took refuge in the attention I got from other men. Like I said, I only lusted for one, but my loyalty to Lock never wavered."

"I see…"

"Bam made a lasting impression on Lock, hence his position as the right hand man. He stood to the right of Lock and Ghost at his left. Ghost, he was by far the worst of the twelve disciples. He wore a permanent frown. His nickname Ghost, was given to him on account of him being the only white guy of the 12. He was as lethal and high-tempered as Lock, if not just a tad bit more dangerous due to his slithering deceitful ways.

Lock and Ghost both spoke with a calming tongue. The right owned up to the responsibilities of a leader, and therefore did most of Locks dirty work. Ghost was a man of many tricks and he carried most up his sleeve. He appeared to be a soldier to Lock, but he wasn't. He was very well camouflaged.

"So what brought you and Bam so close together?"

"Loneliness, he became my companion. A filler for Lock. Once trafficking of the drugs became too heavy, the family started to disassemble. They were scared, and so was their leader. Lock mind fucked me into believing that he was the only man that could touch me. Bam proved him wrong. I mean there is so much to tell, I am sure we won't be able to cover it all in just one session. Besides I am getting sleepy.

"Well why don't I put you under and you tell me a little about some of the incidents that took place."

"Sounds good. I hear you talking, but I don't want to say or do anything that may further incriminate me?"

"Confidentiality clause here my dear." The psychiatrist sat up in his chair and crossed his legs as if waiting for Keyshia to spill the beans. "Try and lay back down, count to 10 and let it all out. Just calmly follow the metal balls and breathe slowly."

Keyshia chuckled slightly at the word usage 'metal balls' as the psychiatrist tamed her puzzled mind just before she fell into a deep sleep.

"So tell me more about the family."

"The family betrayed me. I fed them, and gave them shelter, but in the end they feared me. Turned Lock against me. I somehow, still love them. I will say this.

Lock was right about two things pertaining to business and life. You should never let the emotions override reason, and love will get you killed.

UNDER LOCK AND KEY, HONOR AND OBEY PART 1
AIJA M. BUTLER

I died several times in this manner. I loved him and I would do anything to protect him, only he fought me in every way imaginable. I could feel his love with every blow. The love he tried to overshadow by hate."

"So…, Keyshia." the therapist broke in, with a questionable glare, "So all this took place on campus?"

"Yes on school grounds in my 4 bedroom apartment. Lock forcibly led my roommates away. I wasn't allowed to talk to my friends any longer." Keyshia grew solemn and shook her head as she squeezed her eyes closed tightly. She was desperately trying to shake away the images playing in her head. "All 8 of my roommates were gone like the wind in a matter of a week. Lock's college drug trafficking ring was brilliant, yes, anyone would have to admit that, but it took away my freedom."

"How was the operation carried out? I mean campus police, security, someone had to notice that there were miscellaneous persons touring campus on a daily basis." The therapist looked puzzled and put his hand on his chin tapping his pen with the other."

"Campus police?" Keyshia chuckled. It was like she was in some sort of trance. Her eyes remained closed and she twiddled her thumbs. "The campus police were just as stoned as we were. They bought from Lock and two of them even sold for him. If I wanted to get out it was kill or be killed. You don't just walk out on the Family, unless you were asked to leave; and let me tell you it was either by bullet or 2-3 story drop, right onto the pavement below my patio balcony." Keyshia shook her head. "Campus police. What a crock as for the operation…"

Lock never sold up the hill on campus, just in the dorms. Everyone bought from him, could you imagine 3000 dorm residents blowing your phone up all day, and these students weren't buying a bag here and there they were buying in bulk? College parties, hazing, or just a smash party occurred on a nightly basis. Hell, the students were so fucking high on campus, we all would borrow food or come to one another's place and make a spread, to calm the munchies.

Selling on campus was just a piece of Lock's operation. He was still getting heavy loot from the streets. Lock had a crew selling in his hood and he trapped from nights on end, selling and pulling licks. He was married to money, power, and the life he led by the gun. There wasn't very much room for anything else."

"Anything else like what Keyshia, do you care to elaborate on this."

"Love…, he was like stone, but passionate at the same time. I know it may not make much sense to you. It didn't for a long time make sense to me either. His passions were for money and respect. He couldn't risk falling for me and expressing it."

UNDER LOCK AND KEY, HONOR AND OBEY PART 1
AIJA M. BUTLER

"So this Lock person, was ruler and father figure to these men, and drug supplier to the masses, what was he to you?"

"He was my world…and I was his Queen, honor and obey, my only rule."

THE

BEGINNING

UNDER LOCK AND KEY, HONOR AND OBEY PART 1
AIJA M. BUTLER

9 TO 5

Keyshia tossed her briefcase on her desk and sighed heavily. "I can't stand this job, it must be the money. The hard work is a Bitch and the employees are a pain in the ass. I swear if I didn't have to pay for tuition I'd walk right out the door."

Keyshia threw a stack of papers onto her desk and went into the lounge to make some coffee. She was alone as usual on Sunday's. Though the office was severely quiet she had to admit she rather enjoyed the peace. The sounds of Los Angeles' busy streets hung in the air, "Nothing like the smell of money." Keyshia exhaled.

High heels slapped the pavement and leather briefcases swung in time with the wind. Peering through the 10th floor window Keyshia smiled at her success. Toasting the others on the business strip, she held her cup high and took a sip.

Keyshia began to organize her thoughts. Talking to herself was a normal ritual, it helped her remain in tune with her conscious efforts to make well thought out decisions.

"Well, I guess it's just me today. Sunday, of all days stuck in an office alone making last minute conference calls for the big gala."

Keyshia swung her hips to and fro back to her filing cabinets pulling potential candidates to serve as hosts for the BET awards. The hotel and restaurant business didn't seem to rest. For every award show and after party came the royalties of advertising the company's services, and the intense training of highly sophisticated workers, to represent the company and clients. Hart America set the standard for banquet servers, cooks, and hosts for the most prestigious Los Angeles Hotels.

"Is anyone here?"

"Who's asking?" Keyshia projected her voice from her corner office.

UNDER LOCK AND KEY, HONOR AND OBEY PART 1
AIJA M. BUTLER

"It's Andre' can we talk?"

"Andre'?" Keyshia mumbled quickly trying to jog her memory. Since working for the company, Keyshia had made many male friends, male friends she used for both her business and pleasurable enjoyment. Keyshia enjoyed the attention and flirting was her natural way of communication.

"Hold on I will be right there." Keyshia came around the corner from her office and busied herself at the file cabinet. She purposely didn't make eye contact with Andre', a façade she used to indicate she had no time for casual conversation.

"So what can I do for you, Andre'?"

"You can come here for starters."

UNDER LOCK AND KEY, HONOR AND OBEY PART 1
AIJA M. BUTLER

"Well, I could do that or I could continue to pull these files I must have collated by noon. We have a huge order to fill for the banquet. "

"Stop frontin' and come here."

Keyshia threw her files up into the air as Andre' locked the door of the office. She ran into his arms and gave him a long passionate kiss. Andre' picked Keyshia up from the floor in response to her erotic foreplay and sat her down on the counter of the front office.

"I missed you!" Keyshia slurred in an erogenous manner through parted lips.

"Oh yeah, so why were you trying to act as if you didn't know who I was?"

"Because I am at work." Keyshia toyed with Andre'. "I am trying to keep it professional here in the office." Keyshia smirked at her sarcastic play as she leaned her head back in ecstasy as Andre' kissed her neck and down the front of her chest.

"Are you trying to have your way with me?"

"That depends! Would you like me to, is it just us today?"

"Just you and I baby, for now anyway. I have a few clients coming in and who knows who will come in to pick up their checks."

"You're still handing out funds? Why don't you break me off one?"

"I would if you went to work once in a while."

"I thought you didn't want me to work for the company any longer." Andre' leaned in with his eyebrow raised in question of Keyshia's job inquiry. "Something about the idea of dating your employees bothered you. "Andre' continued sarcastically.

"No! I didn't say you had to stop working. I said we have to stop seeing each other."

"Uh-huh! Well just what are we doing now? You know I am not interested in giving up my freedom or being dictated to keep your job. I call the shots in this relationship."

UNDER LOCK AND KEY, HONOR AND OBEY PART 1
AIJA M. BUTLER

Keyshia was waiting for the punch line to kick in, but it soon dawned on her that Andre' was serious about his position on the matter.

"Jobs come a dime a dozen for me anyway." Andre' stated.

Keyshia pinched her lips at Andre's obvious lie. If that were true he wouldn't have shown up at her office door in the first place. After all Hart America was a temp agency for prominent banquet servers and hotels, but it was for workers that didn't have steady employment just the same. Sure the pay and gratuity was high, but a few days of work here and there at the most.

"No keep this one." Keyshia insisted. "Besides I have some work that I need to get filled today and well, I could use you." Keyshia moved in close and threw her arms around Andre's neck and closed in on his lips. "What do you say?" She teased biting her lower lip for effect.

"What's the pay baby?"

"10 an hour plus gratuity."

"I'm on it, just write down the itinerary."

"Thanks one down, 59 to go." Keyshia shimmied from the top of the desk in an attempt to guide her skirt down from well above her knees, and began to gather the files she had thrown about the office.

Andre' knelt just in front of her to help, gazing at Keyshia's brow for a few moments he continued on in what he knew to be a sensitive subject.

"How's school?" Andre's face was now serious. "Can I come over tonight?"

"No you're working, remember?"

"Well how about tomorrow?" Andre' was interested in finding out what was the problem with him seeing her on campus. Was she seeing someone else? Andre' threw the papers he had recovered from the floor of the front office onto the desk and plopped down in the chair.

Andre' sighed in frustration. "It's just I haven't been able to spend any time with you since the new semester started."

UNDER LOCK AND KEY, HONOR AND OBEY PART 1
AIJA M. BUTLER

"That's because I have a lot on my plate right now baby. I work all day and then I have classes at night."

"Are you still seeing your ex?"

"Well yeah, we are best friends. Is there a problem?"

"Yes, as a matter of fact there is especially if he has been coming to see you and I haven't been able to. You know I'm not trying to have an argument with you, but I need to know where I stand. Every fucking job you send me on this cat is present. If I can't get rid of him, I'm pretty sure you can't. I'm not sure you even want to." Andre' was busy hurling questions Keyshia's way, he hadn't noticed her irritation or lack of interest. "Why do you keep helping him anyway?"

Keyshia raised her eyes from her file as she had desperately been in search of and lowered her tone. "You don't want to go there with me Andre', just let it go. I don't need this right now. Justin has been there for me through thick and thin. I am not going to just tell the man, "fuck you, I have my life in order so you can kick rocks," now that he needs me. I need to at least pay him that courtesy. I had no home and no family. Now he is in need of employment and I am in the position to help so I will do so."

"Yeah, isn't that convenient. Let's not forget you two were high school sweethearts and that you were all in love for four years.

UNDER LOCK AND KEY, HONOR AND OBEY PART 1
AIJA M. BUTLER

Things don't sound as they seem. You say things didn't work out. I say you guys just needed some time a part to get your lives straight."

"I want to continue seeing you, but I don't need the extra drama Andre'."

"You're right babe. Perhaps I am sounding a bit insecure. You know you do a lot of good for these guys that come into the office. Many of them would be in jail if you didn't give them jobs."

"Really now, well maybe someone should send the boss a memo. I could use a raise. You know I had to give up my basketball scholarship. I didn't have time for practice and games with the job and classes."

UNDER LOCK AND KEY, HONOR AND OBEY PART 1
AIJA M. BUTLER

"Well the guys have you to thank for keeping them out of trouble, that's for sure."

Keyshia blushed. "Well this job gave me another chance at finishing school and I am thankful for that. I owe it to my co-worker for putting in a good word for me with the University. I hope I can do well so that I can make her proud. I'm all alone now. I can't go home. I refuse."

"Is that your story baby? Please tell me. I want to know everything there is to know about you. I'm sorry about bringing up Justin. I know that there is nothing going on between the two of you. Just promise me you won't jeopardize our relationship. I know how the ex-boyfriend-ex-girlfriend rule book goes."

UNDER LOCK AND KEY, HONOR AND OBEY PART 1
AIJA M. BUTLER

"Oh really! How is that?" Keyshia lay on the desk in the middle of the front office. Her blouse was unbuttoned and her skirt was hiked up to her upper thighs. Andre' stood right between her legs swaying them from side to side teasing her with his sexy looks.

"What time is it?" Keyshia gasped as he looked frantically at her DKNY watch.

"I don't know babe what time is it?" Andre' continued making advances towards Keyshia not realizing she had regained her senses.

"Shit! Its 11:30." Keyshia leapt from the desk. I have to get these contracts finished by noon. I have a meeting at the Biltmore Hotel. I have to schedule some workers for the Bonaventure as well."

UNDER LOCK AND KEY, HONOR AND OBEY PART 1
AIJA M. BUTLER

"Okay, okay! Keyshia calm down."

"I can't Dre'. It's the awards banquet for God sakes. This company is counting on me, and hell I am counting on this damn job. I'm 20 with a job that pays me a little over $1500 a week. I am used to the Macy's shopping sprees, and catered lunches aside from the soothing feeling of my bills being paid on time. Plus the BMW out front doesn't fuel itself. Please remember that this is also the banquet that you are scheduled to work at." Keyshia slipped her heels on and made her way to the front desk. While gathering her belongings to prepare for her list of errands, the door to the office swung open swiftly. She hadn't realized she'd unlocked it just yet. A moment sooner and she would have been caught in a rather compromising position.

"Hi, oh my goodness you startled me. Can I help you? We aren't open for business today."

"Oh, um…I'm sorry…, um…, the gentleman on the first floor said that this office could get people jobs. Is there a Keyshia here today?"

Keyshia smiled and looked back at Andre'.

"Yes this is Keyshia." Andre' pointed out to the seemingly worried man.

"I know that you are not open today, but ma'am I really need a job. I was laid off and I have two kids and a wife to take care of. Do you think you can help me out? I am not that old and I am in pretty good shape."

"Well I don't know. I am pretty swamped today. I think I can help out, but I will need you to come back tomorrow morning to go over all of the paperwork and necessary documentation."

"Keyshia!" Andre' interrupted. "Don't we have a few job openings right now? I understand you have a location that needs to be filled this evening. I could show him the ropes."

"Yes as a matter of fact I do." Keyshia said giving Andre' a little nudge. But I have some things I have to get done. I don't know that I will have the time to interview you and conduct a proper background check before my next appointment."

"Well why don't you just take care of all the paperwork on Monday? That way he can work tonight, I mean I'd be there to keep a watchful eye on him. Besides he could really use the money."

"You have a point Mr. Johnson. How about it? What do you say Mister….?" Keyshia turned her attention to the solemn looking man lingering at the front desk counter.

"Oh it's Frank. Mr. Franck Milano."

"Famous Italian Bistro Owner Mr. Milano…?" Andre' looked both puzzled and honored to be in his presence.

"Ex-owner, we ran into financial issues and I was forced to sell. My wife is terribly ill."

Keyshia threw Mr. Milano a shaky smile and extended her hand to welcome him aboard. Well okay Frank. Let's get started."

BOY FRIEND UNKNOWN

Keyshia's eyes were growing heavy as she sat on the subway heading back across town to her campus apartment. She leaned her head against the glass and watched the lights and cave walls pass with each stop hoping and praying the train remained on its track. She wasn't used to public transportation, but working in Downtown, LA was troublesome with a vehicle, besides she enjoyed the peace as she rode the bus and train.

UNDER LOCK AND KEY, HONOR AND OBEY PART 1
AIJA M. BUTLER

Keyshia smiled at the thoughts of Andre'. He was new, which was something she needed. A refreshing change, he was there during her time of need. Breaking up with Justin was devastating.

"I wish I felt comfortable with him coming over to the apartment." Keyshia spoke aloud to herself. "I just don't trust any of my horny roommates, and issues with Justin have left me so insecure and afraid to trust men. I am seriously afraid to hurt him and myself in the process." Keyshia whispered to herself tracing Andre's name in the palm of her hand.

"I want to be with Andre' and he seems to be interested in pursuing a long-term relationship. God!" Keyshia sunk deeper into her seat. "I just don't know if I'm ready for that. Andre' was right. There were unsettled issues with myself and Justin. I just don't feel comfortable talking about Justin with Andre' and besides it may push him away. I was only interested in sharing as much as I needed to, in order to keep the relationship afloat.

Keyshia signed and lifted her head when she heard her stop come over the intercom. She was anxious to get home and kick off her high-heeled shoes. Her feet were so sore. She had a mind to contact campus security to come and pick her up from the bus stop and cart her to the campus apartment complex.

UNDER LOCK AND KEY, HONOR AND OBEY PART 1
AIJA M. BUTLER

Keyshia stooped over her to retrieve her briefcase from the floor and escorted herself from the crowded bus and headed up to the campus. Pulling her keys from her purse gave her great pleasure. She couldn't wait to hit the showers and grab something to eat.

"What's up girls?" Keyshia greeted her roommates as she passed through the living room. "How were classes?"

"They were there." Caroline said sighing with frustration.

"Hey do you have classes tonight?" Natalie chimed in. "I have a few friends coming over to chill. I thought maybe…"

"Maybe what!" Keyshia said giving Natalie a 'what now look'.

"Well," Natalie hesitated. "I thought maybe you wouldn't mind chilling with everyone. You know what I'm saying? I mean is like Justin coming over or something?"

"No, but I really didn't feel like being bothered Nat. Especially with your people, Nat."

"Please just this one time." Natalie begged with praying hands.

"Oh please! Whatever Nat that's what you said the last time. What about you Carol, what…you don't want to babysit Nat's boyfriends friend tonight?"

"Nahhh, you know I don't do blind dates. You my friend are a brave soul."

"So, what do you say, please?"

"I seriously do not want to be bothered tonight, and besides you know I have a boyfriend."

"Um Hum." Natalie whispered to Caroline. "Well that remains to be seen."

"And that means what, exactly?"

"Funny!" Keyshia replied and left the room in a hurry.

"The guys will be here in less than an hour, so I will go ahead and free up the shower for you!" Natalie screamed graciously.

UNDER LOCK AND KEY, HONOR AND OBEY PART 1
AIJA M. BUTLER

"Yeah, yeah thanks!" Keyshia yelled back over her shoulder. Keyshia opened the door to her bedroom and free dived onto her bed. "Wow." Keyshia sighed kicking her heels to the side. "What the hell am I going to wear? I haven't done my laundry."

Keyshia scooted from her comfortable position and threw her head back with frustration as she straightened her stance.

"Brit" Keyshia yelled across the hall to her dorm mate as she hurried across the hall as if trying to catch Britney in the act. She was sure she could find something both hot and sexy out of Brit's closet. She was the queen of dance attire out of all the roomies. Well, the girl with the latest fashions anyway.

UNDER LOCK AND KEY, HONOR AND OBEY PART 1
AIJA M. BUTLER

Mommy and Daddy were footing the college bill and she had plenty of left over cash to throw around. Keyshia took advantage of that situation whenever necessary. After all, she and Britney were the same size.

"Hey Brit, can I wear this red number you got here?" Keyshia bombarded Britney's closet without a full welcome. Not that Britney minded. She was too busy rolling a blunt.

"Sure, got a hot date?" Britney looked up briefly from her sticky fingers as she licked the honey seal from her fingers. She was so masterful at blunt rolling it was a wonder why she wasn't majoring in agricultural studies, those that involved drug trafficking and all aspects of government operations.

"No more like a blind date, one of Natalie's doings."

"You know Keyshia, you should tell her that she can't just keep assuming that you are going to be home and that you will be able to entertain her boyfriend's friends, not cool." Britney carefully placed her 10th blunt into her pink jeweled case. "Oh, hey do you want to study later. We have that big quiz on Friday and I know we both need to pull an A or high B in that man's class. He is such an asshole."

"Yeah he is, I do need to hit the books. Thanks for asking. I will knock on your door when I get rid of my unwanted guest."

"Ok I will be up!"

FRIEND

OR

FOE

He was in the apartment one morning, a friend of Brit's. I'd seen him once or twice around campus, but I didn't care to know him. He wore long surf shorts, a t-shirt, and sandals. His hair was cut low and his mustache and beard were untamed. He stood as Keyshia entered the living room area, as if startled. His guitar fell to his side.

"Does Brit know you're here?"

"No!"

"Hum, are you supposed to be!?"

"Well if I weren't I wouldn't be just standing here as though I am embarrassed to be caught in someone else's apartment so early in the morning, without warning. Caroline let me in on her way out."

"Ah, I see. Well, can I offer you something to eat? Brian isn't it?"

"I don't mind if I do, and yes it's Brian." He replied, he wasn't shy at all.

"How do you like your eggs? Over-easy, scrambled, or what?" Keyshia bit hungrily into her granola bar, finally looking into his face. Brian nervously shifted in his seat.

"Beggars can't be choosers."

Keyshia agreed and laughed slightly. It doesn't matter anyhow. We're having left over pizza."

Brian smiled. "That's even better."

"Well at any rate you are on your own. I will have mine cold I can't afford to be late for work. Microwaves on the counter, help your-self.

"See you around." Brian smirked.

"Not likely." Keyshia looked wide-eyed and gave Brian the cue to come and handle his business in the kitchen. Keyshia didn't have any time for small talk. She excused herself from the kitchen and sashayed to her bedroom to gather her belongings. Keyshia knocked on Britney's door to let her know she had company. She didn't want him to help himself to the other food items in the pantry or clear out the refrigerator all together.

Keyshia was impressed by his musical ability's. The guitar was a beautiful golden brown with gold strings. He looked like a panhandler. All he needed was a sign. Brit said he attended the University. That was a big surprise. Keyshia was disgusted at her recent attraction to the rogue. His untamed beard made him oddly attractive. Keyshia grabbed for her briefcase and bolted for the door trying not to eye Brian on her way out.

****

Work had ended and Keyshia couldn't think of anything more relaxing than a shower and a book. No phone calls and no company.

"Shit." Keyshia muttered as she spotted him. Well actually she sort of ran into him, as she was trying to look as if she was studying the material for her psychology quiz the following week. Keyshia was red in the face, which embarrassed her farther and caused her ears to turn red and burn.

"Oh, I didn't see you there."

"It's okay."

"Brian right?" Keyshia squinted while pointing a finger and tilting her head.

"Dinner." he implied.

Keyshia looked around unsure if he was talking to her. She didn't know this guy from Adam. How could she just jump up and go out to dinner with him? Besides she was more than interested in who was going to pay for this meal, considering his attire hadn't changed from whence she first met him. Although it was the same day she couldn't imagine parlaying around campus in the same outfit she'd worn all day at work. The steam of the shower was calling out to her.

"Are you okay?" Brian was staring at Keyshia waiting for a reply.

UNDER LOCK AND KEY, HONOR AND OBEY PART 1
AIJA M. BUTLER

"Yes!" Keyshia hit her head in befuddlement. "Yes, yes, sorry let's go." Keyshia blurted in her animated and embarrassed tone. Keyshia had a problem saying no to people. She was always going beyond the call of duty to keep others happy. "Where's your car?" Keyshia looked puzzled.

"I don't drive."

"Oh, okay." Keyshia dragged on and rolled her eyes. "Well maybe we should take a rain check on dinner? I just got off of two buses and a subway to get home. I couldn't take another minute of public transportation."

"It's not far. I wanted to take you to the Mexican café just down the hill. They have the best burritos. Cheap too, I guess they take pity on us college students."

"Well in that case, let's go. Cheap is my middle name presently." Keyshia lied she shopped at Macy's during her lunch break and ate out on the regular. She was starving, and couldn't wait to order her a nice super-sized burrito filled with beans, cheese, and rice, extra salsa on the side. Perhaps some freshly fried chips as well. Keyshia's stomach began to growl. The lights to the Mexican café comforted her as they approached the door.

Brian opened the door, and ushered Keyshia to a table near the window. The view wasn't bad at all. The University was situated in the hills just outside of Pasadena. Tall trees, woodsy bark, and the smell of pine, often reminded her of her summers in Yosemite she spent with her family, camping and fishing within the wild. The college didn't seem to differ much. Out in the wild, fit the scenario and wild coyotes graced the campus apartments and classroom area on a regular.

Brian was talking about his entire life, Keyshia imagined as she daydreamed about her burrito. He talked about his band and their tour in Brazil, which was fascinating. They were in a talent show, and chosen to be one of the acts as part of the college tour. The tour in Brazil would last for 6 months. He and his friend were excited about the opportunity because the scholarship would help pay for their classes next fall. The tour would take place during the spring and summer.

Keyshia finally chimed into the conversation as her thoughts drifted to lands abroad. "Six whole months in a whole new country, I'd kill for a chance to participate in something so great. Being a part of the student's abroad program is so rewarding. The opportunities are endless. Keyshia's eyes brightened as the young Hispanic male brought over her burrito. She could still see the steam rising from it.

"This looks good." Keyshia commented as she spun her burrito around in search for a nice place to attack her prey. Keyshia dug into her burrito trying not to appear like she was starving as much as she was. After tasting it her eyes grew wide with surprise and disgust at the same time.

Brian laughed as Keyshia picked over the items in her burrito. "What's the matter? Is something moving?"

"No, but I'm not quite sure what kind of meat is in this thing." Keyshia paused and leaned her head down towards her plate to get a closer look.

Brian smiled at Keyshia's inquisitiveness. He delighted in her slight irritation and worry. "Let me taste it, I am a wiz in Latin American cuisine."

Keyshia spun her burrito over to Brian allowing him to cut a sample and test it out. Brian chewed for a while and moaned agreeably.

"This is cow tongue."

Keyshia gaged as she tried to keep herself from panicking, "What!?"

"Keyshia, are you okay?"

"I didn't order this." Keyshia said angrily.

"Oh I think you did."

"I don't eat cow tongue. I think I would know if I ordered a cow tongue burrito," Keyshia said disgusted trying not to throw up on the table. Keyshia swallowed hard. "You can't be serious Brian.

UNDER LOCK AND KEY, HONOR AND OBEY PART 1
AIJA M. BUTLER

"It's okay. You can order something different. What would you like?"

"Okay, most definitely something without meat, say beans, cheese, and rice. "

"Sure I think I can manage that," Brian commented confidently.

Keyshia was so hungry by the time the burrito arrived she couldn't hear a word Brian was saying. She managed to throw in an occasional uh huh, hum, that's nice here and there. Brian was looking at Keyshia scarf down her burrito. She hadn't noticed the silence.

"You must be hungry."

"Mm, yes/" an adlib was all she could muster with a mouth full of beans and tortilla.

UNDER LOCK AND KEY, HONOR AND OBEY PART 1
AIJA M. BUTLER

"Keyshia, Keyshia!" Brian alerted as he was talking to seemingly himself for the better part of the date. He had long since caught on to her nonchalant responses.

"Oh my God, I wasn't listening I know. I'm so sorry. I just got so hungry watching you eat. It was torture. I was beginning to think that the cook had to travel back to Mexico to fix my burrito.

"Ha…ha…ha, cute…very cute," Brian found Keyshia's company to be very liberating. He enjoyed her smile and her conversation was well worth the time. Thank you."

"No thank you."

"For?"

UNDER LOCK AND KEY, HONOR AND OBEY PART 1
AIJA M. BUTLER

"For dinner, silly"

"Well, I was returning the favor."

****

Brian walked Keyshia back to campus and up to her apartment. No one was home from classes yet. So she had the shower to herself. Her psychology quiz was on Friday so she decided that she would take a stab at the material.

Brian stood at the door of the apartment and looked inside. "It's pretty dark in there do you want me to stand guard while you get settled in?"

"Thanks but, you don't have to do that. I should be fine. Besides," Keyshia stopped as her key was in the door smiling at her next statement. She was teasing and she knew as much. "I think if someone were here it would most likely be one of my roommates. " Keyshia gave Brian a smug grin she knew full well that her hard shell was melting away.

"Okay well how about I just come in to keep you company for a while." Brian suggested. Unwilling to take no for an answer,

"Sure." Keyshia stated. Keyshia didn't feel like company, her spontaneity already set her back a few hours. Her feet were hurting she had been on them all day. Keyshia didn't really want to be in the apartment alone with some guy she just met, but Keyshia had a problem with saying no.

UNDER LOCK AND KEY, HONOR AND OBEY PART 1
AIJA M. BUTLER

Even if she couldn't do what others were asking of her, she often agreed to comply with their requests.

Brian kicked off his flip flops and sat his guitar in the corner, of the living room. "So you don't mind if I stay and keep you company? Do you have any plans? I don't want to impose."

"Plans?" Keyshia looked in the sky replaying her activity's she'd planned for the evening before his intrusion. "Oh no not really," she lied. "I was just thinking about doing a little studying. I have a quiz on Friday and a term paper due in two weeks."

"Oh you have plenty of time."

UNDER LOCK AND KEY, HONOR AND OBEY PART 1
AIJA M. BUTLER

"Nah, it's my senior year/" Keyshia looked confused and frustrated as she wrinkled her forehead. "This term paper is damn near a book, 60 pages minimum. It comes between me and graduation for damn sure."

"Calm down!" Brian pleaded holding up his hands to beg for mercy on the court. "I hear you sister."

"How about you, what year are you planning to graduate?" Keyshia began to interrogate.

"Well, I would be graduating this year. But I chose to study abroad for a year. They have a five year program for those who wish to get a Masters in International studies. The band is a perk."

UNDER LOCK AND KEY, HONOR AND OBEY PART 1
AIJA M. BUTLER

"I see." Keyshia replied feeling like she had been out shined and quite embarrassed for the hostile line of questioning. "It sounds interesting. So what is your first love, the music or the foreign policy?"

"I would have to say the music, but the foreign policy is what will feed me and my family. Well at least that's the plan. I suppose it isn't too late in the date to ask you if you are seeing someone." Brian took a stab at changing the subject to a more personal aspect.

"No, not at the moment." Keyshia lied. It was the easiest thing to do. Her present love life was far too complicated to discuss. "If I were in a relationship with someone, I wouldn't be entertaining you. I don't have time really. I work all day and have classes at night. I have met a few men on campus and I've had about a dozen dates in the last few months. My ex and I are best buds and he is always here so that could have something to do with it as well. It kind of puts a damper on things. What about you, are you dating anyone?"

Brian ignored the question about his love life and lack thereof to delve deeper into her ex-boyfriend business. It seemed that all of Keyshia's potential mates had qualms with Justin's continued presence. "So what is the deal with you and your ex?" Brian wrinkled his forehead.

"Honestly, I'm not sure. We were together for a very long time. We are comfortable together and sometimes that's enough. You know what I mean?" Keyshia was looking for understanding because honestly she wasn't sure about things with Justin herself.

"So, is it serious with you and your ex or not?" Brian questioned with an inch of added bass to his smooth voice. He was obviously getting far too irritated about a matter that truly hadn't much to do with him. They had a burrito at a local café.

"It's serious, but we are not a couple." Keyshia retaliated.

"How am I supposed to take that answer? I mean is there room for a relationship or are you tied down?"

"Okay what is this Brian? Was dinner a date or were you returning a favor, because your line of questioning is starting to sound like a jealous boyfriend. I don't want you to feel as if I am misleading you or something. Possibly you are looking for something else."

"Yeah I'm interested and no I didn't set you up. I just find you extremely attractive and fun to be around. I haven't had that in a while. Just interested to know where you stand. Do you suppose maybe you would be interested in exploring a new fling?"

"Well Brian, that's just it. I don't really want a fling. How did we get on this subject anyhow? None of this really matters."

"I think that it may just matter, now answer the question."

"If I were interested in someone I would be willing to pursue a relationship, not a one night stand or fling as you put it."

"Understood, and your point is well taken. So, are you going to show me your room or what?"

"Just as long as you know that we are just touring the apartment. It's not an invitation."

"I can respect that."

UNDER LOCK AND KEY, HONOR AND OBEY PART 1
AIJA M. BUTLER

Keyshia showed Brian down the hallway for a tour of her room. Keyshia's bed was full of satin and fur decorative pillows. She had a tall palm tree that reached as high as the ceiling. Her big screen television was mounted on the wall. Her computer sat on her desk next to a container of pens and pencils. There was a 50 gallon fish tank sitting on its own stand close to her bed filled with different color fish, under a black light. On the night stand to the left of the bed was a fancy beaded lamp that resembled some of the throw pillows on the bed and floor. Keyshia had two beanbags on a bed of fur, which was her area rug, just in front of her entertainment center.

She had everything. None of Keyshia's dorm rooms had ever resembled the drab look of the college dormitory, not even her freshman year at Loma Linda. Brian looked around the entertainment center viewing all of her delectable treats. Keyshia had a video game system, a VCR/DVD player, and a nice radio system. Keyshia had even made it a point to get her own blinds and curtains. The stock blinds were dusty and old fashioned. Keyshia threw out the splintered desk that once occupied her space and traded it in for a nice $100 desk from office max. Brian couldn't believe his eyes.

"Your room looks like an apartment in itself. I especially love your bed." Keyshia had a queen size bed. It damn sure hadn't come with the apartment. Keyshia never kept a roommate for long. They were either too nasty or didn't respect her space. Brian kept eying Keyshia's bed.

"Your bed is beautiful, the colors are nice and I bet it's nice and soft." Brian slid his hands along the soft silk of the colorful spread with great intentions. "Who drew all these pictures?"

Keyshia had a habit of hanging her work on the walls of her room. She always signed them creatively and put them in glass frames. Everyone that visited her room assumed that she was an art major. The truth was art wasn't at all her passion it was an ability she would just rather forget she possessed. She was far more interested in the works of the mind.

UNDER LOCK AND KEY, HONOR AND OBEY PART 1
AIJA M. BUTLER

"I did. I drew the pictures. It's nothing really just something I do in my spare time, which is less and less these days."

"A guy in my band is an art major, he is pretty good, but so are you. "

"Wow, thanks for the compliment. Perhaps I will meet him one day."

"Yeah we call him the karate kid. He is a black belt in martial arts, and is currently teaching me. I'm a brown belt. I am up for the black belt soon. It is a sport that is well disciplined. I recommend it to procrastinators."

"Really, what an assessment, I hadn't thought of it in that sense. I do believe that the study of martial arts teaches a little bit about temperance."

"Well, well, well, aren't you somethin' lil mama?" Brian gritted his teeth and sniffed and snorted like a bull dog. Keyshia was visibly disgusted.

"Weeellll?" Keyshia dragged on with a questionable tone in her voice.

TOO MUCH

TOO SOON

Keyshia turned her gaze over to the clock. Her eyes were beginning to grow heavy.

"Wow, time as flown. It's getting late, and I have to wake up in the morning for work. I'll escort you to the door. Maybe I will see you around. You know, if you decide to come and visit me again. Keyshia was speaking fast and with very little breaks to ensure Brian had no room to object. Keyshia began to trot down the hallway towards the front door, purposely avoiding his response.

Making no eye contact, she reached for Brian's guitar. Keyshia slowed her pace when she realized the silence and stumbled back to her room to find Brian standing where she had left him.

Brian looked down at his feet and spoke with a humble calming tone. "Do I have to leave? I was hoping that I could stay here with you." Brian put his hand up quickly to stop Keyshia from responding. "Before you answer the question I want you to know that I am not trying to take advantage of you. I just enjoy your company. I know that you're tired, and I don't want to keep you up."

"Brian!" Keyshia started in, but Brian continued.

"I can sleep. We could just lie together and have pillow talk until we fall asleep."

"I don't know Brian, Keyshia said raising an eyebrow. "It's risky don't you think?"

"No, I told you I won't try anything."

"I wasn't referring to you. I don't want to take advantage of you, either. I don't see any harm in sleeping." Keyshia pulled her robe from the back of her bedroom door and headed for the shower.

Brian looked around Keyshia's room examining the drawings on the wall and the characteristics of her room. He opened her closets to see how tidy they were. He was happy to find that they were fairly neat, but not perfect.

"Good," he sighed to himself. "At least there is one thing wrong with her." Brian was afraid that Keyshia may have been too perfect. He needed to find a flaw. Still, he was worried about how soon he had become infatuated with her. Brian shook away the thought of making advances on Keyshia, as he smelt her perfumes that decorated the top of her mirrored dresser.

Brian made himself comfortable. He had retrieved his guitar from the living room and placed it on the other side of the entertainment center. Then he lay on the fur rug just in front of the bed because he wasn't sure how she felt about people sitting on her bed or rearranging her living space.

Day dreaming about how she looked with her hair down, or the way she moaned during orgasm, or how peaceful she looked while in slumber. Brian could feel his love rising, as he gazed at the ceiling in Keyshia's room. He dimmed the lights and turned on some music to set the tone and waited for Keyshia's return.

****

Keyshia took her time in the shower. For some reason she trusted Brian. She felt no need to hurry or hide her belongings. Keyshia couldn't shake the idea of her new found risk taking personality. Thus far, her life thrived on stressful times, planned events, or doing favors for other people. By the time Keyshia stepped from the shower, she made up her mind that she wouldn't hold back if sex was to present itself. She didn't want to use him for sex, though.

Keyshia wiped the fog from her mirror and viewed her reflection, "Okay girl you can do this. You're beautiful and single. Well tonight anyway. So let something good happen to you. Stop worrying about everything, just be you."

Keyshia reached for her lip liner, but shrugged and tossed it aside. She decided she didn't need any make-up. He seemed to be attracted to her natural beauty. Keyshia put her robe on, and tossed her work clothes into the hamper just inside her bedroom door.

UNDER LOCK AND KEY, HONOR AND OBEY PART 1
AIJA M. BUTLER

Brian appeared to already be sleeping. Only the light from the aquarium was on. Keyshia took off her robe quickly and put on her red satin nightgown.

Keyshia kneeled down and planted an innocent kiss on Brian's cheek, trying not to disturb him, but when she pulled away, Brian suddenly grabbed Keyshia by the waist and placed her gently on top of him. He moaned softly and speaking romantically, he explained how he couldn't resist.

Keyshia touched his face and trailed her thumb across his soft lips. Keyshia forgot about any reservations she had with Brian and went with the flow. She liked the fact that she could just take control of the situation and she didn't have to throw hints in the air for him to make a move on her.

Brian's hands groped and moved in time with the music. He'd found a slow jam compilation amongst her CD's and thought that it would be nice to have some music playing, a refuge from the uncomfortable silence.

Brian wasn't interested in conversation anymore, anyhow. He wanted to score with Keyshia. He was infatuated with her mind. Brian wondered whether their chemistry would take them beyond friendship.

Keyshia dug her fingernails into Brian's back in ecstasy. Brian followed suit by pulling his shirt over his head in one movement. He was so smooth she hadn't realized that she was wearing little clothing herself. Her night gown was lost in the wind.

Keyshia began to get into the rhythm of things and started to let herself go. Brian coached her through and encouraged her to be vocal about the ways in which he made her feel. She was reluctant to sound off and call out his name. She was afraid she would sound fake...So in her nervousness to calm down she chickened out and pushed away from Brian's blissful passions.

"I can't do this."

"Sure you can. You were doing just fine. Baby, just let yourself go. Don't try so hard. Do what you feel. Don't be afraid I won't hurt you."

"It's not that Brian. It's just that I just met you. I barely know you. I have no idea what your last name is. How old you are, I mean what are your intentions after we make love? Do you consider this making love or just sex? Please don't get angry."

"I'm not angry, Keyshia I'm disappointed and frustrated."

Keyshia rolled off of Brian and lay parallel to his body. She covered her face with the palm of her hand, and laid there in disgust for a moment. She had never been one to do the straight fuck and go deal. Andre' weighed heavy on her mind. She was filled with such frustration as to why she didn't trust that Andre' was right for her and that he wouldn't treat her the way Justin had.

UNDER LOCK AND KEY, HONOR AND OBEY PART 1
AIJA M. BUTLER

Truth was she had to get things straight with Justin. He was her High School sweetheart. His actions, however were beyond forgivable.

Justin's betrayal ran deep, it was wasn't just the cheating, his abusive tongue, and later physical show of tyranny. It was the fact that he knew her through and through. Her abuse prior to dating him at the hands of a man when she was a child, how she opened up to him.

Months and months she was tormented with the dreams of her attacker while Justin was peeling back the layers of insecurity to deflower an innocence that was already gone. STOLEN, at the tender age of 8, sex was a complete chore, and Keyshia had yet to know the feelings of true love and/or making. She was fearful of sex and that was a major turn off for the men she met. She usually just faked it, but something was different about Andre'. Something that scared Keyshia so bad that she was running as fast as her legs could carry her.

"Keyshia, KEYSHIA!" Brian's voice escalated at Keyshia's unresponsiveness.

"Huh!" Keyshia was clearly in her own world and hadn't truly heard a word he said, if he said anything at all prior to yelling out her name. "What is it?" Keyshia answered softly.

"Don't beat yourself up about it, Keyshia. If you're not ready I'm not going to force you to do something that you don't want to."

"No, Brian it's not that I don't want to. It's, I'm just not sure it's you is all. Is this a serious thing? "Keyshia cut her eyes his way to see if he was buying her sob story.

"Keyshia I don't have issues with being with you on a romantic level, you do. You are the one with the emotional baggage, and by that I mean you are still heavily involved with your ex-boyfriend. I myself don't know how to deal with a situation like that. I think that it could get dicey, so maybe it's your conscience warding off my advances. Look, how about just forget about sex and cuddle for the rest of the night. We can lay and hold each other through the night."

Keyshia signed in relief and accepted his change in plans. Keyshia reached for her red satin nightgown. It came across the shoulders and down to a deep cleavage, falling dangerously close to the nipple area. Brian began to kiss her tracing the cut of the gown with his lips. Brian took a deep breath and failed to exhale. She was lost in lust.

Again Brian removed the gown, "What are you doing?" Keyshia spoke nervously.

"I want to feel skin next to mine. You won't be needing the nightgown. Don't worry I just want to be close to you, if you will allow me."

UNDER LOCK AND KEY, HONOR AND OBEY PART 1
AIJA M. BUTLER

Keyshia felt beautiful. She hadn't a care in the world at the moment. Keyshia's hair was all over her head her satin nightgown was crumbled in a corner. Keyshia pulled on her red lace boy cut underwear and her matching tank and snuggled under Brian. She had no regrets concerning her encounter with Brian. In fact, she was looking forward to a new day.

UNDER LOCK AND KEY, HONOR AND OBEY PART 1
AIJA M. BUTLER

ALONE AT LAST

Keyshia stepped out of the shower and wrapped her towel around her body. She cleared the fog from the mirror and admired her reflection. She was well rested and figured she'd get a jump on the next day by cooking and preparing her work clothes.

Keyshia was so tired after work that she skipped class for that evening. A buddy of hers would be sure to give her the notes from class. She hadn't missed a day of lectures since the beginning of the semester. Keyshia threw on her old and faithful grey sweat shorts and half sweat shirt top that hung off her shoulder. It was her favorite lounge outfit. It was comfortable and sexy. The top was cut just above her navel which showed off her belly button ring.

Her shorts hung dangerously low and her feet were freshly pedicured. Keyshia didn't wear much make-up. Her face was plain with a clean after shower glow.

Keyshia walked into the kitchen to start her dinner and was startled by the two gentlemen sitting at the bar. She quickly regained her composure and handled the introductions.

"Keyshia, and you are?"

Bam bit his bottom lip, while staring at Keyshia. "Bam!"

UNDER LOCK AND KEY, HONOR AND OBEY PART 1
AIJA M. BUTLER

"Nice to meet you, and you are?" Keyshia rose an eyebrow and looked at the gentleman on the right. He was quiet and showed very little expression. He was stone cold. Her hand froze as she reached out to greet him. Mr. Man fixed his eyes on to hers and simply winked.

"Mr. Cool! Ma main man, how do you do? Does this mean I don't get to know your name?"

"It's Juju."

"Nicknames huh, are you felons?" Keyshia laughed playing in her sink full of bubbles. She got no response. "So what are you guys doing on campus? Juju you don't look a day older than 16."

UNDER LOCK AND KEY, HONOR AND OBEY PART 1
AIJA M. BUTLER

Bam was looking over Keyshia's shoulder, but quickly turned his attention to Keyshia.

"Yea what's up!?"

"I asked what the two of you were doing on campus, visiting perhaps girlfriends, brother or sister?"

"No not necessarily, business is our pleasure." Bam smiled.

Lock had long since drifted into the hallway and caught sight of Keyshia. He was visiting a client. One of Keyshia's roommates. He was listening in as Keyshia teased his companions. Lock stood in back of Keyshia silently and ordered the guys to keep his presence a secret. Lock smirked and gestured a simple, "Um hum," clearing his throat, before wrapping his arms around Keyshia and planting a kiss on her neck.

Keyshia's eyes grew wide and her face and ears became red and hot with embarrassment. Lock's associates began to laugh. Keyshia, playful and flirty herself spun around with a huge grin.

"Ummm, who are you?" Keyshia said with sex in her voice, as she wrapped her left over chicken.

"What! No dinner, I mean it smells terrific."

"I'm sure it does, but by the looks of that leather jacket and platinum watch you'd rather have fillet mijon."

Lock smiled, "Cute, very cute. It's Lock. I thought I would just stand back and watch you from afar. Did you find out all you wanted to know? I see the three of you were playing twenty questions." Lock looked unnerved as the two gentlemen were sitting at the bar uncomfortably.

"Well no actually. I only got to ask two or three questions, and I didn't get to ask you any." Keyshia said caressing the edge of her shorts, exposing a sneak peek at her palm tree tattoo became of great interest to Lock.

"Bust a…what does your tattoo say? I can see the palm tree."

Keyshia lowered her shorts so that he could get a better glance at the picture and logo. It was a palm tree with a coconut that had fallen from it which read, "Bust a nut."

"Bust a nut, huh!" Bam and Juju were more than excited. Juju was making obvious gestures to Bam about the sexual innuendos that the tattoo suggested.

Lock traced the outline of the palm tree seductively, "Sexy!"

"Thanks!"

"You are a beautiful and intelligent young lady. I choose you." Lock announced.

Keyshia wrinkled her forehead taken back by his forwardness. "What?" Keyshia replied in a puzzling and sarcastic way. "I guess I should be flattered?" Keyshia commented hesitantly. "Do you have some sort of super powers which allow you to forecast future happenings?"

"I hope I haven't insulted you in some way, if I did it wasn't my intention." Lock replied.

"You haven't." Keyshia ran her fingers through her long flowing curls.

"See you around."

"I'm sure you will."

Keyshia's eyes followed Lock right through the front door. She was anxious to find out from Natalie exactly who Mr. Lock was and the nature of his business.

Keyshia found herself daydreaming in class and rushing through assignments at work just so she could return home and await a possible appearance. He said, "I choose you." Keyshia twiddled her thumbs as she looked through her music library, so that she could dance away her frustration.

Brian had come by every day since their romantic encounter. She wasn't sure what to make out of their relationship, but she knew that after meeting Lock thoughts of him stood in the way of anything blossoming with Brian.

Keyshia wiped the sweat from her brow and shed her clothing. Stepping into her robe, she retreated to the bathroom for a nice cool shower before drifting to sleep in her cold satin sheets. The water fell so clear. It fell from under the showers head into a great

UNDER LOCK AND KEY, HONOR AND OBEY PART 1
AIJA M. BUTLER

water fall. Keyshia peered through its glimmering drops to find her eyes fixated on the diamonds of her ring shining so brightly. She was surprised that she was still wearing her engagement ring, she rolled her eyes and blew into the air as she remembered she was wearing her ring in the presence of Lock. "I wonder if he noticed it?" Keyshia shook her head shamefully. *No matter anyway*...Keyshia's thoughts drifted.

The engagement was called off over six months ago, but Keyshia couldn't bring herself to take off the ring.

Keyshia rinsed quickly and nervously rushed from the shower. She burst into a panic reliving the night of Lock's appearance. Removing the ring from her finger she sighed with relief and tossed it into her cosmetics drawer.

Keyshia stood at her long mirror just in front of her bedroom door. She'd just begun to love herself after such years of abuse in her previous relationship. He hadn't hit her physically, but the mental beatings and unfaithfulness, had done severe damage to her trusting others and self-esteem.

Keyshia began to lotion her body and slipped on a long t-shirt. The night had turned into the early hours of the morning, but her mind wouldn't rest.

Tamia was singing in the background and just as if Lock could read Keyshia's mind he appeared into the red light of Keyshia's room.

UNDER LOCK AND KEY, HONOR AND OBEY PART 1
AIJA M. BUTLER

Stepping into the room he quietly closed the door. Keyshia fell into a small coma unable to respond to the presence of Lock. She didn't know how to deal with her emotions. However she wasn't confused. She was very eager to get Lock alone.

Keyshia looked hungrily at Lock and motioned for him to come closer.

"Damn I have been waiting for you. "Keyshia whispered.

Lock took his shirt off immediately. The moment Lock's shirt hit the floor Keyshia fell from her seat in the window and flew into Lock's arms. Lock grabbed her and pulled her close. He kissed her passionately, mumbling how beautiful she was while kissing down her neck.

Her sex was wet, her morals began to slip, and her self-control diminished. Keyshia's shirt mysteriously disappeared as Lock picked her up from the floor. Lock cleared the dresser with one sweep and sat Keyshia on top of the mirrored dresser and leaned Keyshia back against the glass. She moaned and begged for more.

Lock wrapped his hand around and inside the cream of her thighs and entered her soul. They fit like a key to a lock; as their passions joined together as one.

****

UNDER LOCK AND KEY, HONOR AND OBEY PART 1
AIJA M. BUTLER

The next day he moved in. Keyshia stood in the middle of her bedroom smiling blissfully at the crumbled sheet on her bed. Her comfort pillows were thrown about the room alongside their clothing. Lock was in the living room with his boy's discussing the day's venue. He wanted to get the boy's more involved with their schooling and find jobs.

Keyshia leaned onto the bar area of the kitchen. "Can I offer you boy's some breakfast?" Lock smiled and leaned in to give Keyshia a good morning kiss.

"Good morning sweetie. Breakfast would be nice, but we have to pass." some of the boy's looked disappointed. Lock was admired and respected by the boys. He possessed a power that Keyshia found intriguing.

Lock was very much like a big brother. Bossy, moody, and everyone else did the chores.

"Babe, we have some business to take care of." Lock hinted.

"Oh, okay." Keyshia sounded a bit embarrassed. "Well, my men have to work don't they? Hey I'm just going to hop in the shower and get ready for class. I have two today. I should be back in time to make some lunch should you get hungry. What time do you think you will be home?"

"I'm not sure I'll call."

"Okay that's fine. I'll see you later." Keyshia smiled brightly and headed down the hall towards the shower.

UNDER LOCK AND KEY, HONOR AND OBEY PART 1
AIJA M. BUTLER

THE FAMILY

Although Lock had a college degree, the street life still had a hold on him. Lock ran major drug sells on every block on the East side of L.A. He'd graduated college a year early with a degree in business. His plan was to start law school last fall, but his mother fell ill and he was forced to take care of his younger brother and sister.

He literally led two lives. Lock was also a Crip. Those that followed were also members of his gang. He had a vision and he was going to see it through even if the consequences ended his life. I too, accepted the challenge and became a member of the Family.

UNDER LOCK AND KEY, HONOR AND OBEY PART 1
AIJA M. BUTLER

LOCK HIGH ON KEYSHIA

It turns out that Lock was right about his choosing Keyshia. He'd done quite a bit of research. Keyshia's roommates indulged Lock's interests in Keyshia and her history.

Keyshia was a scholar with a very dangerous mind. She had honorable discharge from the United States Marine Core, which was said to be classified information. She was two quarters away from a bachelor's degree in Psychology and Criminal Justice; and was well known for her dissertation on serial killers. The now

UNDER LOCK AND KEY, HONOR AND OBEY PART 1
AIJA M. BUTLER

published works received both negative and positive reviews.

Keyshia felt that the serial killer was in everyone. A ticking time bomb, just didn't know who, when, or if it was going to blow. During her research she found that most serial killers and mass murderers were regular people living in stressful situations. People overcome tragedy through coping mechanisms, but if the support isn't there and if the stress levels are too high, you are likely to blow. Keyshia also sited that a lot of child and women killers had developmental issues and childhood problems. Mother's that allowed their Father's to put the book down once he had gotten a hold of the piece. It was graphic in nature and some even said that it was grotesque as if she were one of the ill sickened minds.

Lock found great use in Keyshia. Her writing told small truths about herself and she seemed fragile as well.

****

Lock insisted on leaving three of the disciples on guard 24/7. He was over protective and with good reason. Lock was a dangerous man. He was also feared, but those in high places reign only for so long. So he was careful to educate Keyshia on the ways of the streets and the importance of watching each other's back.

Lock had an apartment of his own, but he felt safer there with Keyshia. He could remain focused on the tricks of his trade rather than those that perhaps hunted him. Certainly, others begged to differ, a few in Lock's entourage felt that Keyshia was a distraction and the left especially felt it was important to maintain a distance between sex and love relationships. Keyshia felt the lines as her presence was more common in meeting and governing ventures. She understood, but the division among family members worried her.

There were 12. The twelve disciples later became the Family, Lock was the King and Keyshia took her place as Queen. The right hand was also newly appointed and it obviously upset the left. The right hand walked Keyshia to and from classes. She enjoyed him. He was quiet, but very intelligent when he spoke. All twelve of the disciples were hand-picked by Lock and well trained.

They developed an organization that would not only promote the Family's survival, but the opportunity for growth and advancement. Lock was willing to stand down when it came time, and revenue was evenly split amongst the group.

So came the birth of a Family, which was celebrated by this creed:

"I welcome you to this vessel of sworn identity, FOR LIFE. Although as we raise our glasses to toast our new commemoration, I say to you Key and the FAMILY, repeat after me.

UNDER LOCK AND KEY, HONOR AND OBEY PART 1
AIJA M. BUTLER

This Family may grow and with each member, everyone must follow protocol. Respect the Queen. Respect one another, and remember you can be erased." Lock rose his glass initiating a toast.

"To the Family." Lock recited.

"To the Family!" The Family replied. The family's echo rang loud and clear. Following a roar of laughter applauding their riches.

UNDER LOCK AND KEY, HONOR AND OBEY PART 1
AIJA M. BUTLER

SHOWERED WITH GIFTS

Keyshia heard the front door open from her bedroom. She had been lying in the dark for what seemed to be hours. Furious with Lock, for leaving her home alone for such long hours. Her anger dissipated however, the moment she heard his keys. She began to blush.

Keyshia scurried to put her glasses on in the dark and fumbled to turn on the lamp on her nightstand. With one motion she grabbed for her book and lecture notes, and dove right into a studying frenzy. She was suddenly, cramming for midterms. The truth of the matter was that she had been so preoccupied with Lock and the family, she rarely studied. It was a wonder why the Professor hadn't dropped her for excessive absence. Teachers couldn't deny that Keyshia could miss days and still pass an exam with flying colors.

Lock came into the apartment grinning from ear to ear. He took his gun from in front of his pants and laid it on the side table on his side of the bed, and began undressing.

"What are you reading, babe?" Lock inquired leaning in for a quick kiss. He was busy hanging his leather bomber and placing his money in the safe tucked away in the closet.

UNDER LOCK AND KEY, HONOR AND OBEY PART 1
AIJA M. BUTLER

"Oh, some crap for my Forensics quiz."

"Is that right?"

"Why yes it is." Keyshia looked up from her glasses hanging at the edge of her nose. She gestured for Lock to come close patting the space next to her on the bed.

Lock began crawling from the foot of the bed towards Keyshia. Keyshia quickly closed her book and tossed her glasses aside.

Grinning enormously she started to run. Lock caught her in mid-air rustling her done to the bed playfully. Keyshia and Lock laughed and giggled wagering on who would get to be on top.

UNDER LOCK AND KEY, HONOR AND OBEY PART 1
AIJA M. BUTLER

"What happened to my rose?" Lock asked spotting a few loose petals scattered on the floor.

Keyshia bit her bottom lip and lowered her eyes. Unsure if she could play with the issue. "How do you know they were for you?"

"Don't play!"

Keyshia paused and tensed her muscles a bit to prepare herself for a possible blow to her stomach. Lock was good for that. She searched his eyes. He was so hard to read. Keyshia often fell into confrontation trying to gage his reactions to her sarcasm.

"I threw them away since you took so long getting home." Keyshia's mouth smiled, but her eyes looked worried.

"Oh! So you call yourself getting mad and trashed the place?"

"Sort of!" Keyshia shrugged, flinching when Lock lifted his hand to touch her face. "I'm not now." Keyshia smiled talking in her phone sex voice.

"Oh you're not huh! What's for dinner?"

"Me!"

"Do we get dessert?"

"Nope!"

"Well I do!" Lock reached for his bag.

"Watcha got there?"

"Close your eyes."

UNDER LOCK AND KEY, HONOR AND OBEY PART 1
AIJA M. BUTLER

Keyshia clapped her hands in anticipation of her gift. Her heart was beating fast and hard. She was brave in that moment to trust Lock and his plan of action. She held so much fear in her heart of Lock she'd become paranoid and took to drinking quite heavily. Something Lock despised, but failed to notice how his actions drove her to it. Her drunken stupors helped to numb the pain.

Lock always had gifts, even before the beatings started. At first, Keyshia didn't expect them. Only after Lock's tantrums did she expect some sort of reconciliation in the form of material luxuries.

Just a few weeks before, Keyshia was going on with her ex-roommate Britney about needing a car. The next evening Lock took Keyshia out to dinner in a car he said he rented for the occasion. As Keyshia and Lock left the restaurant, Lock dangled the keys Keyshia's way and told her to drive home.

Keyshia was just excited to even drive the car.

"Wow! I get to drive home." Keyshia was cheesing so hard, her smile glistened brighter than the 4ct. diamonds in her ear.

"It's your car, why shouldn't you drive home?"

"What! Oh my God! Keyshia jumped up and down ecstatically. Keyshia ran to Lock, as she wiped away her tears. "I love you, Lock."

****

UNDER LOCK AND KEY, HONOR AND OBEY PART 1
AIJA M. BUTLER

Keyshia sat up staring into space, her head slightly to the side smiling softly.

"Keyshia."

"Keyshia," Lock yelled.

"Yeah!"

"Where were you? You seem pre-occupied by something."

"I'm just reminiscing. You been so good to me. Enough already. What's in the bag?"

"Close your eyes," Lock demanded. Lock unzipped the bag and started pouring the contents all over Keyshia. Keyshia screamed in excitement and gasped for air. She grabbed a handful of money.

UNDER LOCK AND KEY, HONOR AND OBEY PART 1
AIJA M. BUTLER

"Oh my God, Oh my God, Oh my God! Keyshia repeated hysterically. "How, why, who?"

"Because I need and want you in my life. This is for us babe? This is our family. It's our chance at doing something big."

Keyshia grinned and shook her legs in a dramatic display of her joy. In that moment it didn't matter much that Lock had yet to speak of love. He always said things like, ***I love the way you think, look, and feel.***

Though Keyshia longed to hear those sweet word of love, his desires were evident. Since money wasn't a factor. The two of them could concentrate on the betterment of their relationship.

UNDER LOCK AND KEY, HONOR AND OBEY PART 1
AIJA M. BUTLER

Keyshia looked up from her fixation on the pile of money before her. "Have you ever made love on a bed full of money?"

"No!"

"Do you wanna?"

"Sounds good, but the possible tearing of my bread just made my shit go soft and I was hard as a rock. How about we just toss the money around the room and make love in the ambiance of it all?"

"Perfect."

Lock climbed on top of Keyshia and ran his fingers through Keyshia's hair. Keyshia closed her eyes and allowed Lock to control her as Sade played in the background. She wanted desperately to take control and show Lock how good she could make him feel, if he'd just relax, but even in bed he feared letting go of control.

Lock's love making was stiff and aggressive. Keyshia would catch him slipping into a passionate slow grind. When she did so she'd urged him to keep going. Her acknowledgement made him stop. His thrusts became hard and rough. Keyshia wanted desperately for him to take notice of how good love could be. Instead, she settled for his presence.

Lock sexed Keyshia until the light began to peer between the blinds in the bedroom. Keyshia's body was intertwined with his like a key to a lock. The sun brightened the complexion of their bodies, as they submerged in loves bliss.

UNDER LOCK AND KEY, HONOR AND OBEY PART 1
AIJA M. BUTLER

The

Fog

THE UNSPOKEN TRUTH

UNDER LOCK AND KEY, HONOR AND OBEY PART 1
AIJA M. BUTLER

Keyshia's room was filled with smoke. Shadows of the 12 disciples and the King lingered in a blue light, as she walked amidst the men in her heels and red dress. Keyshia held close a glass of her usual alcoholic. "Pink Panty." beverage starring Lock down as she approached his throne. The men were busy at work. Piles of weed and coke covered her desk and bedside tables as they were being weighed and bagged for sale.

Keyshia was drunk again and Bam could tell she was heavily intoxicated as she weaved about the room seductively. His heart came up through his throat as he fixated on Keyshia in hopes she would look his way.

UNDER LOCK AND KEY, HONOR AND OBEY PART 1
AIJA M. BUTLER

"Damn it Key." Bam thought to himself, he more than loved Keyshia he was obsessed and would kill for her. He was tired of Locks malicious ways. Lock was the one who drove Keyshia to drink. She had no escape and the only thing she could do to cover up the scars was to become numb to the fact. He only wished he could save her. Though he betrayed Lock as his right hand, falling in love with Keyshia wasn't hard to do. She had a way about her.

It was Lock's loss, scared to love Keyshia the way she deserved for fear he would lose power and respect. Bam felt that power and respect was demanded, and earned. To lead by example would prove the power of his leadership. Lock was too smart for his own good in Bam's eyes. He was

UNDER LOCK AND KEY, HONOR AND OBEY PART 1
AIJA M. BUTLER

stupidly listening to the one man of his colony that wanted him dead. The same man he called his best friend, one he grew up with, and got jumped into the same gang with. King, Lock kept his enemy unknowingly extremely close.

Keyshia was down for a show. With each sip of her liquor courage she approached Lock as he sat in her desk chair and leaned in close to his ear. Locks nose began to flare at first sight of Keyshia and her outfit. He was both disgusted and turned on. Keyshia nibbled on his ear and slipped her free hand down to the zipper of his jeans and grabbed his manhood seducing him to take her right there in front of his men. After all he loved to make a show of his control over her and his troops.

Bam's chest was beating so hard his muscle tee slightly jumped at the same rate as his heart. Ghost watched contently the display awaiting the drama to follow. Lock didn't take too kindly to public displays of any kind unless he initiated it.

In an attempt to take back control, Lock grabbed Keyshia by the neck knocking her glass to the floor and warned her about making a public spectacle of herself. Keyshia threw her head back and laughed. She was a gross sight, a beautiful drunken woman shamelessly stumbling about the room like a cheap whore.

Lock was becoming more embarrassed by the moment.

"I told you about that bitch." Ghost interjected. "She can't even hold her liquor and you got her holding the loot like she trustworthy."

Lock let go of his grip on Keyshia and threw Ghost a warning stare for disrespecting the Queen. "You keep her name out of your mouth. I will deal with her. She belongs to me."

"Oh how are you going to do that, Lockkkk…?" Keyshia chimed in laughing and slurring her words, and enunciating his name.

"Stop!" Lock warned her again about her philandering tongue. He warned Key about her drinking on several occasions. He needed her to keep a level head. He counted on her to have his back, but he dare not mention it aloud. Lock was scared of his men, he knew in his heart that Keyshia was right about them. They were lying in wait to take his spot. He was paranoid and uncertain of who to trust. Lock looked at Keyshia as if he were looking into her soul. The truth of the matter was that he knew he had driven Keyshia to drink. She wasn't a drinker. She was broken.

"Stop." Lock said, only this time with a leveled calm tone.

"Why Lock? I am just doing what you do." Keyshia dribbled in a drunkenly sarcastic slur. Losing his patience Lock grabbed Keyshia's arm and twisted it, and snarled a murderous threat through a smiling face and clenched teeth. Keyshia moaned erotically though she was in extreme pain.

"You had better get it together. I am going to forget that this little incident happened." Lock leaned in close to Keyshia's cheek and lowered his eyes as he investigated her body. "You been giving my pussy away, Key?" Lock asked as he watched Keyshia's upper lip perspire. He knew that Keyshia's intoxication brought out unspoken truths.

Silence fell over the room. Lock let go of Keyshia's arm to light his blunt. He took a deep and long hit and blew the smoke into Keyshia's face. "I asked you a question." Lock stated stepping back from her and folding his arms as he took in another hit.

UNDER LOCK AND KEY, HONOR AND OBEY PART 1
AIJA M. BUTLER

Bam stepped forward just behind Keyshia as she looked to be leaning slightly, he grabbed Key by the arm and turned her towards the door to escort her out of the room. "I will take her to the shower." Bam interjected as Lock looked at Bam with a displeasing glare.

Bam damn near drug Keyshia outside the room. He slammed the door behind him, angrily. He couldn't wait to lay into her ass. Bam's firm hold on Keyshia's biceps began to infuriate her.

"Bam what the fuck? You are hurting me!"

"You need to get a fucking grip." Bam pulled Keyshia close to his chest. He wanted to take her right there in the hallway, but he knew better than that. "I can't keep you safe if you keep egging this man on. Key you gotta stop drinkn' boo."

Keyshia stood looking Bam deep into his eyes and then rolled them casting away his words of wisdom.

"I know you're tired. So am I. I know you can't handle too much more of this shit and neither can I. I am with you if you want to walk away. I promise, because this shit you doing now, drinking and instigating shit, is gone get us both killed. You are killing yourself and murdering me. We can pull the plug and walk away."

"Pull what plug?" Lock interrupted. Neither Bam nor Keyshia heard him step out into the hall. His gun was drawn. He had his hands in front of his manhood holding the gun right in front the zipper of his jeans.

Bam still had a hold onto Keyshia's biceps, and since Lock's appearance his grip was much tighter. Keyshia's arm was turning visibly red and her hand was beginning to grow numb. Bam didn't budge nor did he speak.

"Don't you think you should remove your hands from around my girl's arm?"

Bam didn't budge or show signs of fear or obedience. Lock wrinkled his brow slightly shocked at Bam's insubordination.

Keyshia interjected, "Bam its ok."

UNDER LOCK AND KEY, HONOR AND OBEY PART 1
AIJA M. BUTLER

Lock shifted his gaze from Bam and began questioning Key about the nature of their conversation.

"I was just telling her to be cool, Lock. I didn't want to see her get hurt." Bam spoke out of term and in place of Keyshia.

Locked smiled in disbelief and shook his head as he toyed with the barrel of his gun. "Hurt by who, Bam?" Lock snickered, licking his lips and flexing his tatted arms.

Bam looked at Lock and then down at his gun, to acknowledge that he too carried a loaded weapon. Bam was clearly out of his mind, Lock concluded, but Bam felt as though he had to protect Keyshia. He didn't care about having to fight Lock. In fact he wanted him to make a move. Keyshia put her hand over her mouth to restrict her vocals, which was an obvious show of guilt and instability. Though she was sobering fast her mental devices were still on hold.

Lock tilted his head slightly allowing for some of his goons to pour out of the smoke filled room and stand guard on each side of both Bam and Keyshia. The hall was beginning to close in on them fast. Key stood just between the hall and the opening to the bathroom, and thought long and hard about bolting and escaping through the adjoined room of her ex-roommate.

Lock holstered his gun and retrieved his knife from his right pocket. The men grabbed on to Bam's arms. Keyshia was afraid Lock was going to stab his own right hand man. Her eyes began to well with tears.

"Lo…Lock…baby why don't we all just go to sleep. It's been a long day. I am sorry I was drinking." Bam still had his hands bound to Keyshia's, as Locks men had firm hold to his arms. Keyshia encouraged Bam to go ahead and let her hand go. She would be just fine.

"Let go of her Bam." Lock starred up at Bam.

Bam withdrew his hand, but encouraged Keyshia to come and stand just behind him. He realized that Lock's goons were still surrounding him as they too let go of him, but he was still reluctant to allow

UNDER LOCK AND KEY, HONOR AND OBEY PART 1
AIJA M. BUTLER

Keyshia to be left alone with Lock. Key looked confused at which way to go.

Bam smiled slightly and shook his head. "Keyshia." Bam called out. Keyshia stood stiff as stone with a blank face.

Look motioned towards Bam and looked deep into his eyes. "Do you want to die?"

Bam just stared.

Lock continued to scold him, "Don't you ever disregard something I have told you to do. I understand you care about the Queen's wellbeing, but you would do best to remember that she belongs to me, and so do you." Lock put his knife up to Bam's neck and tested the fear in his heart. Bam stood tall and looked up towards the ceiling. Keyshia became so angry with Bam she wanted to kill him herself for disobeying Locks orders. She was so afraid that he would kill him then she would truly be alone.

Keyshia winced a bit as she threw her arm out to Bam in an attempt to advise him to stop the madness. Lock smiled. He took Bam's silence for bravery and removed the knife from his presence.

"Well, its good you have no fear. I guess that is why you are my right hand man. Just remember…" Lock paused and took a step back from Bam and hit Keyshia with a closed fist straight in her mouth.

Bam yelled, calling Keyshia's name as she flew into the bathroom, sliding across the tile floor and hitting her head on the sink.

UNDER LOCK AND KEY, HONOR AND OBEY PART 1
AIJA M. BUTLER

Lock cheesed at Bam as he fought to break free from Lock's goons. "I want you to remember something. That…" Lock pointed into the bathroom at Keyshia laying on the floor. "Belongs to me. I truly hope you understand what I am saying. I won't repeat myself, and there won't be another warning. I left you here to protect what's mine. I applaud you for standing up for what you think you believe in, but the line is drawn here. When I am home, I am King and you are one of my disciples."

Bam gritted his teeth and tried to stay calm as he looked Lock in the face. He was so angry he could feel the burn coming in his throat.

UNDER LOCK AND KEY, HONOR AND OBEY PART 1
AIJA M. BUTLER

Lock turned his attention to Keyshia, who lie bleeding on the floor. "Don't you ever lie to me again. Do you hear me?" Keyshia nodded in response, crying carefully through her swollen and split lip.

Bam's eyes began to fill with tears. Lock dismissed the goon's and patted Bam on his chest as he walked past him. "I got work for you to do later. Don't worry about Keyshia. Oh and by the way, don't you ever put your hands on my woman again or I'll kill you." Lock said.

Bam just watched Lock's mouth he couldn't hear the words. He read his lips, but didn't respond. All Bam could think about was how he was going to kill Lock. Little did Lock know, the same applied for him as well.

UNDER LOCK AND KEY, HONOR AND OBEY PART 1
AIJA M. BUTLER

Bam had plans to put his own crew together. He couldn't just sit around and wait on Justin any longer. Shit was about to get real. Bam straightened his stance and buckled towards the front door. He needed to get some air. He desperately wanted to whisk Key up from off the bathroom floor to tend to her, but he didn't want to make matters worse for her at the present time. He blamed himself for her most recent blow from Lock, but he had, had enough.

Lock eyed Bam, as he walked towards the front door. "Aye, you want in on this domino game bro?"

Bam turned around straight-faced and scanned the entire room and left the apartment without a word.

Lock just laughed and shook his head mumbling, "Bitch ass niggah."

10…9… 8…7…6…

Keyshia sunk her sorrows in a bottle of wine as she soaked in the tub. Her body ached from Lock's last beating. The swelling in her face had gone down just enough for her to return to work.

Keyshia was hurting so bad she could barely get her arms in the sleeves of her blouse. Her clothes were all too big, and her hair had lost its luster. Just a week before she was forced to cut it low to about 3 inches and wear her natural curls. Lock loved her new look. Unaware she was forced to change her style due to the stress of the Family.

Keyshia spun around in the mirror. She looked frail. Still her make-up was

UNDER LOCK AND KEY, HONOR AND OBEY PART 1
AIJA M. BUTLER

flawless. She fought back tears, worried about how she was going to tackle work and classes effectively. Lock had slipped a bit in his beating tactics. Usually she was well covered by trousers and long sleeve blouses that hid her scars well.

In addition to the war at home. Lock slowed on paying some of the bills. Another reason why Keyshia was forced to go back into work. A place where she once loved. Now, she spent most of her time hiding and avoiding personal questions about her livelihood.

Keyshia enjoyed the ride on the subway to work. Her mind wandered. In the moments of her approaching her office building, all logic seemed to seep through her brain and drizzle like wax from her ears. It was like maggots had infested her brain. There was nothing audible. There was nothing more than a long beeping noise. Her senses were delayed. Her shirt was buttoned haphazardly. Her skirt was turned sideways. The seam and split was in the front. Keyshia's hair was lacking oil sheen, her natural curls were beginning to develop small dreads. Keyshia was losing it.

As Keyshia walked down the long road to the office. She made plans for an escape. She knew she wasn't going to be able to continue working for Hart-La.

Keyshia barged into the office, spilling her coffee all the way to her desk. The owners an older white couple looked on to the scene with worried eyes. They were more like parents to Keyshia. Keyshia had been alone in Los Angeles. She took care of herself. Up until now, Keyshia was doing an awesome job for a 21 year old, now eligible to club and drink. Terry walked up to Keyshia and placed her hand on her shoulder.

Keyshia was sitting at her desk just staring into a blank computer screen. Keyshia was so startled she flinched. She jumped up from her chair and knocked the coffee all over her computer and files for the Biltmore Hotel banquet. Keyshia was so embarrassed by her clumsy behavior, she grabbed her briefcase and mumbled a few incoherent apologies as left the office, never to return.

****

UNDER LOCK AND KEY, HONOR AND OBEY PART 1
AIJA M. BUTLER

"You ready?"

"Lock, I'm so tired. Do we have to do this now?"

"We do! How do you plan on protecting yourself in the event I am not here? Bam won't be here much longer."

"What is that supposed to mean?" Keyshia looked up from her kneeling position to look Lock in the face.

"I think he has over-stepped his boundaries a bit don't you?" Lock was staring down at Keyshia, as she retreated her glance from his eyes, to the floor. Lock came around to face Keyshia. "You're my girl right? You know how much you and this Family mean to me. I need you to focus. Bam is my right hand man. He will be out in the field, more so now. I need to make sure you can handle yourself on your own."

Keyshia was stunned by Lock's words. She knew exactly what he was talking about. She dare not utter another word. It would just upset him more and set him off.

****

Bam couldn't stand that he left Keyshia there alone with Lock, for fear the beatings would just get worse. Bam was so afraid that Lock was going to kill Keyshia. He just wanted her out of there. Leaving her made Bam feel like less of a man, but he just couldn't stay in the same vicinity as Lock anymore. It was just a matter of time before the show down would commence.

****

The red bandana was wrapped so tightly around my eyes that my head was both hurting and beginning to perspire. I was afraid. Not because of the task at hand, but quite frankly at the consequences if I failed the mission. It wasn't like the camp in Virginia at all. I sat amongst tall trees, in uniform, cleaning and assembling my weapon strategically and without error. Only this act of wars preparation was both degrading and another show of Lock's control.

Lock studied my profile carefully and planned his attempt to woo me. His plan worked, I was strong in defense, but weak with emotion. I wanted love, the love he couldn't give, but he could fake it. He wanted to make sure what I had accomplished did not over shadow what he could do to me as a man. He wanted to mentally destroy me.

****

"Count to 10." Lock stood over Keyshia with his gun drawn flexing his tatted arms and chest.

'Focus, tell me the steps you are going to take to dismember in 5 and 5 to place back together.

Keyshia's palms began to sweat, and her heart beat fast. Her breasts were

UNDER LOCK AND KEY, HONOR AND OBEY PART 1
AIJA M. BUTLER

beginning to show beads of sweat as they pushed from under her sports bra. Keyshia played with her tongue ring as she always did when she got nervous. She inhaled hard and fast and held it there for just a few moments before letting it out slowly.

Keyshia could feel Lock's breath on her neck. The fear began to settle in her throat. The lump nearly choking her. She was sure he was going to do bodily harm.

Keyshia closed her eyes and took in a deep breath, "10…., three steps…, unscrew top, hold the butt of the gun not the barrel…9…, press finger in notch right under the screw, spin it slightly and pull it out… 8… pop barrel off…7….2 notches inside barrel-press both and separate barrel of gun

UNDER LOCK AND KEY, HONOR AND OBEY PART 1
AIJA M. BUTLER

from the butt….6…," Keyshia felt around on the floor for her mini screw driver, in order to separate the trigger piece away from the butt of her gun. She started to fumble a bit as Lock hovered over her whispering threats into her ear.

Lock kicked the screw driver from in front of Keyshia, "You're running out of time. You call yourself a marine? The men need you and you can't even put your weapon together." Lock pointed the barrel of his chrome 9mm to Keyshia's left temple. "It's do or die."

"Lock, I'm trying." Keyshia whimpered nervously shaking as she couldn't find the bullets to her gun. She skipped separating the trigger and began to put her weapon back together.

"30 seconds." Lock chimed into Keyshia's concentration, as she desperately tried to venture into the confines of her dark mind. The plan to ignore Lock's presence wasn't working at all. She was failing her mission and just assume give up. This first test was loyalty, the second respect, now discipline and action.

"TIMES UP!"

Keyshia tensed her muscles and hung her head.

"Lights Out!" Lock commanded as he hit Keyshia across the head with the butt of his gun. Keyshia didn't make a sound she just fell over like a tree cut from its root.

UNDER LOCK AND KEY, HONOR AND OBEY PART 1
AIJA M. BUTLER

DO OR DIE...

The blood rushed to Keyshia's head as she jumped up from her laying position and grabbed for her 9mm tucked away under her pillow. The room was black as night and her motions were that of a ninja preparing for the attack. Keyshia reached down slipping her hand into the top of her nightstand drawer to retrieve the extra bullets for her small nickel plated 25, but she quickly tossed away

UNDER LOCK AND KEY, HONOR AND OBEY PART 1
AIJA M. BUTLER

that idea for fear she didn't have time to make sure the gun was loaded and ready to go.

Lock had always kept guns in and around the apartment's perimeters in case of an emergency. Living in fear wasn't an option in Lock's eyes, it was kill or be killed so preparation was a must. Keyshia could hear the footsteps approaching from far down the hall of her dorm apartment. Nervous and unsure of what her next move would be she double checked her fire arm. It was pitch black, but she knew and made love to her killing machine often. She would never disrespect or mishandle it. She relied on its protection.

UNDER LOCK AND KEY, HONOR AND OBEY PART 1
AIJA M. BUTLER

Keyshia's heart was racing, beating so fast she nearly passed out from the adrenaline rush. It was like a damn movie, but the reality settled deep into her bones and the idea of kill or be killed wrapped around her body and caused her muscles to tense.

She was enraged while awaiting just 'who from the family had the balls to come and kill her.' Lock would do better to do it himself. Finally, grow some balls and take care of his own enemy. Keyshia's thoughts ran wild.

Come on Lock." Keyshia whispered to herself. "At least look me in my eyes and pull the fucking trigger."

UNDER LOCK AND KEY, HONOR AND OBEY PART 1
AIJA M. BUTLER

It was kill or be killed. She had nothing left. He had stolen everything. She was gone in her mind, psychologically fucked and ready to die, ridding her soul of all the malice that had infested her heart.

Keyshia wiped the sweat from her brow and stood straight in her tank and boy-cut underwear. Her hair was cut low. Due to the stress of King Lock and his followers her long locks had fallen onto her pillow. Lock thought her new look was flawless and he loved her, but he couldn't and wouldn't dare let her know that.

The bitch in him had erupted into a ball of insecurities that derived from both Keyshia and the Family. Listening to the very man planning to take him out.

UNDER LOCK AND KEY, HONOR AND OBEY PART 1
AIJA M. BUTLER

"Everyone wants a shot at the top and most die from making tedious mistakes or by the very hands of the flock." Keyshia's accusations burned through Lock's chest. He wanted to trust and love her so much, but he wouldn't dare allow himself to fall victim to the pussy. He would be found dead for sure. Lock knew that there may be a mole, in the Family and another plotting to kill him. He was the King how could he not know? Whether he chose to admit that he knew because of Keyshia, would be another story. She was the key to his heart, but to unlock it would prove to be dangerous.

"My bad for telling my King the deceptive ways of his troops. Mere peasants, can't believe the gall of them to flip on the

UNDER LOCK AND KEY, HONOR AND OBEY PART 1
AIJA M. BUTLER

Queen... disloyal than a muthafucka after I'd fed them, clothed them and gave them shelter." Keyshia mumbled to herself as she waited for the door to open. The keys ripped by the doorknob like someone was trying to jam them inside the hinges as if they didn't have the appropriate key.

Keyshia could hear the laughter and a few voices behind the keys and again sounds of someone jamming the keys into the door as if whoever was trying to open it was running from an assailant. The fear of becoming a murderer began to flood her chest and well into the back of her throat threatening to choke her. She no longer feared death since death was an inevitable fact.

UNDER LOCK AND KEY, HONOR AND OBEY PART 1
AIJA M. BUTLER

Keyshia stood her ground as the shadows appeared into the black of her room outlined by the dim light of her hallway. Lock opened the door wide to Keyshia's room, stumbling and staggering in. He was in a drunken stupor.

"Hit the lights." Lock ordered.

Lock was both startled by the lights unveiling and thrown into laughing so hysterically that it brought tears to his eyes, "What the fuck you doin' baby?" Lock asked as he ordered his goons to drop the loot onto the floor next to the bed.

Keyshia was not amused. She still held her gun drawn like she didn't know the men that had trampled into her room.

UNDER LOCK AND KEY, HONOR AND OBEY PART 1
AIJA M. BUTLER

"Baby, it's me lower yo' fucking weapon please. You scaring Ghost." Lock said snickering. He was high as fuck. "Look at ma baby Bam, she wit the shit. You need to get you a lil bad one like this here. She go, and retro, ready to do or die. You feel me? Come here Key. Come and see what Daddy got for you."

Bam was furious. He simply stared right through Lock as he talked about the monster he'd created standing in fear and obedience with a gun ready to fire at whim. Bam wanted to run over to Keyshia, wrap her in his arms and pull her to safety. Sure Keyshia was a well-oiled machine, but she deserved to be loved as well. All that she did was to please Lock and that burned the hell out of Bam.

Keyshia heard Lock's request, but she was reluctant still to lower her weapon with all the drama around the Family. Lately, she was unsure of who to trust. Keyshia was sure she was being set up and she would have to fight for her life.

Bam was staring at Keyshia trying to get her attention, but she dare not look upon his face. Keyshia quickly snapped into her role and grabbed for her robe before Lock took notice to her indecency.

Ghost and Bam began unzipping the bags and pouring the contents of the duffle bags onto her fur rug. The money fell from the four large bags endlessly and covered both the bed and floor.

"What is all this, Lock?" Keyshia inquired as the wads of money began to cover her rug. "What the fuck?" Keyshia yelled as she noticed the blood on J's shoes. "What happened? What did you do?"

"Key," Lock interrupted Keyshia's line of questioning. She had obviously forgotten who was in control of the situation. Her reign was legit as long as she remained a silent partner. "Enough with all the hysterics look at this money. Didn't Daddy tell you that he would take care of you? You don't have to go back to work. I understand it's a good job, but look at all this money. Now, do your job. Start counting and rubber banding this shit up. We need to make another drop."

Bam looked at Keyshia with an intense look of worry as he watched Key's lips tremble slightly. "I'll help her. You two go ahead and drop off the ya-ho. Keyshia and I can handle the weed bagging and money."

"Good!" Lock looked back at Keyshia and told her to come stand close to him. "Put some fucking clothes on will you?" Lock barely moved his lips, but his words were loud and clear. Keyshia grabbed hold of her robe that was once freely open and blowing into the blades of the fan.

"Yes Lock."

UNDER LOCK AND KEY, HONOR AND OBEY PART 1
AIJA M. BUTLER

"Bam, watch my Queen, and hit me with the money count. If the boys come by and the weed is ready go ahead and give them their seller's deal and an eighth donation as a smoker's bonus. I don't want them dipping into the bundle. You feel me?"

"Yeah. I hear you."

www.ingramcontent.com/pod-product-compliance
Lightning Source LLC
Chambersburg PA
CBHW071459040426
42444CB00008B/1411